BREAD OF THE MOMENT

Bread
of the
Moment

poems

DAVID SANDERS

SWALLOW PRESS / OHIO UNIVERSITY PRESS
ATHENS, OHIO

Swallow Press
An imprint of Ohio University Press, Athens, Ohio 45701
ohioswallow.com
© 2021 by David Sanders

To obtain permission to quote, reprint, or otherwise reproduce
or distribute material from Swallow Press / Ohio University Press
publications, please contact our rights and permissions department
at (740) 593-1154 or (740) 593-4536 (fax).

Printed in the United States of America
Swallow Press / Ohio University Press books are printed
on acid-free paper ⊗ ™

Library of Congress Cataloging-in-Publication Data

Names: Sanders, David, 1955 March 4– author.
Title: Bread of the moment : poems / David Sanders.
Description: Athens, Ohio : Swallow Press / Ohio University Press,
[2021]
Identifiers: LCCN 2021011154 (print) | LCCN 2021011155
(ebook) | ISBN 9780804012331 (paperback ; acid-free paper) |
ISBN 9780804041188 (pdf)
Subjects: LCGFT: Poetry.
Classification: LCC PS3619.A5263 B74 2021 (print) | LCC
PS3619.A5263 (ebook) | DDC 811/.6—dc23
LC record available at https://lccn.loc.gov/2021011154
LC ebook record available at https://lccn.loc.gov/2021011155

Passing through the world
along the rooftop of hell,
we look for flowers.

—Kobayashi Issa

CONTENTS

Two

One

Watching the train go by behind
the barren trees, you thought it wasn't
enough simply to see it pass,

you ought to know what's on board.
You looked at the cars for evidence:
cattle, chemical, something else?

What's in those boxcars? you asked yourself.
Empty, full? The squeal of the wheels
against the rails rounded the bend.

The speed, also, was a clue.
You were unsure and so you guessed.
Let's say your guess was right:

how would you adjust your view?
You cast your gaze to the downed trees
that littered the woods, an orange fungus

inching up their trunks like embers,
jewels against the gloom. Somewhere,
barely audible by then, the train.

Because the canary was very young—
if not exactly hardly hatched,
a novice when it came to song—
its owner, also new to the endeavor,
followed the pet shop steps for training.
She kept it away from the kitchen hearth
and left it in the living room winter light,
where it listened alone in its cage to the record
she played, pulling from the reaches of heredity
the array of notes rendered by flute
with Wurlitzer accompaniment.
Finally it started its full-throated singing.
What it trilled was nowhere near
the waltz's tune, but rather the faintest
of approximations, the way a child,
hearing the indecipherable words of the world,
shares a slurred babble of its own
with an invisible friend. The bird sang
and sang at the record's prompt. And its owner,
stirring a steaming pot over the stove,
was as pleased as any parent when she heard.

If the city demands
too much of you,
it pays to pay attention.
Even given the right-

of-way, obeying the light,
you can be yanked
out of your shoes.
Don't dare gawk

at the glass-plated bank
that stands there doubling
your vision of everything—
where even your own

rippling reflection
is waiting to walk—
it can drag you down
the street and run

you over, knock out
your teeth, shatter
your humerus bone,
and that's if you're lucky.

A stray moment is all
it takes, as you know:

a luminous thought,
an unfamiliar voice

shouting hello
from the opposite curb,
the truck at best a blur
out of the corner

of your eye, and you,
too plucky and small
for it to heed. The size
of the place doesn't matter.

Although we were in Florida,
it was November, so it wasn't hot.
Still, the morning of my sister's wedding
we found my father in the motel tub,
where he had evidently spent the night,
clutching his sheet and pillow, pajama clad.
It really wasn't that much cooler there.
He was sobbing, but it sounded like laughter.

You might have guessed it was the thought of giving
his daughter away or maybe something cruel
my mother had said to him the night before.
But it seemed more than that, a confluence
inside him like a bird trapped in a flue
with no hope of escape, beating against
itself in desperation. I had never
known him to cry like that. Breathlessly.

I've felt within myself that welling heave,
which asks for nothing less than my surrender,
and wish, now that I've passed his age that day,
I could tell him so. The suffering of birds
is another thing, and dwelling on it
doesn't lessen it. It magnifies.
In any case, by breakfast he was mostly fine,
and the day a celebration, otherwise.

To stumble into the glare of an afternoon:
that's what's chilling. Adjusting to the sun
while bearing the vessel of your last two hours
out into the streets, where tedium
intrudes without motif or variation . . .
You've bought into a temperament and, blinking,
carry it like a cane that you no longer
need. It looks so good on you, you think.
Spring days in Philly I stalked the old city
before my evening shift began, the soundtrack
rumbling as from the El train or a dream.
Passersby paid me little heed,
clandestine camera, shadowing them
until they turned a corner and I picked up
the stride of the next. This was the point the two
stages convened, unsustainably.
Whose story is this? Whose do you choose?
Like any dream, the one begins to wither
while the other safely asserts itself.
Block by block, bit by bit, I lost
my marquee billing, my walk-on part reprised
in that same old script with the widower on a bench
feeding pigeons and squirrels on the green behind
Independence Hall, the buses wobbling
over the cobblestones, tourists in tricornered hats,
soft pretzels in hand, taking pictures of it all.

As with the woman who hears
the man in the dark
whisper that he loves her
while she pretends to sleep,
the economy of emotion
is worth considering.

If by accident she encounters
Baudelaire in the marketplace
asking for the bread of the moment,
this will give her pause because,
as someone recently explained to her,
a baguette begins to die immediately
and only has, at most, five hours
to make its appeal . . .

Consider, then, the appeal
of this house of stairs.
Some things might stop you
stepping up to step back down
into the sunken rooms:
a sudden back door, a full-length mirror
at the bottom of the landing,
a black kimono on the wall,
a fireplace with piano, a stretch
of hallway ending at the foot of an old bed.

In the house of stairs
she sits in her rocking chair,
embroidering a day-old muffin
into crumbs that she lifts to her lips.
Her keys sing like soft tambourines against her robe.
When she hears the snap of the trap
in the basement, she knows
the bait has found the mouse,
and then she waits
for the death to cool,
to stop its work and rest
before she collects it.
She clutches her keys in her fist—
a brass bouquet—to keep them quiet.

He dared himself to force the door.
Once in, he maneuvered room to room
past outdated kitchen appliances,
shrouded couches and porcelain figurines,
and radios at room temperature.
Sunlight chewed through the drapes' dry rot.

But as soon as the pipe, the calabash bowl
of burnt sienna, found the boy's hand,
he scooped it from its resting place,
a drawer long closed, which he had opened,
in this house abandoned by the heirs of its owners,
and slipped it into the pocket of his pants,

then glided out to his waiting bike that took him
coasting past the corner filling station,
the church, the town hall, downhill
toward home, his eyes tearing
in the whistling wind, and kept it
hidden among his worldly possessions
for most of the rest of his life. *His pipe, not his pipe.*

When the boulder slid off
the hill behind the Armory,
I was in bed a mile away

reading back issues
of the *London Review of Books*.
I'd heard nothing,

but it crushed a car
and came to rest beside
somebody's poor front door.

No one was hurt. Heavy rains
must have pried it loose
from the soil. Neighbors claimed

it sounded like thunder. Then they saw
electrical sparks and thought:
Fireworks! The folks inside

the house watching TV
said the slide felt to them like
"a mini-earthquake." No doubt.

Bleary-eyed partiers uptown
hopped from bar to bar.
And if the car horn

blaring from on high
registered with any of them,
it only implied

that a distant alarm
was riding the spring night air.
Neighboring homes were evacuated.

It weighed about a hundred tons,
city officials estimated.
Someone could have died.

Daily, denizens walk past our window—
ours and others'—and down the street
like jeweled mechanisms in a clock.
At some point they make their turn,
climb the hill, and head toward
their dead-end lane, no matter
the weather or season. Likewise,
in the spring, particularly, we've gone by
their neat Cape Cods and have glimpsed
a cat in front of the curtains of one
and a few times have caught
a silhouetted head against
a flickering screen in another,
before the sun had truly set
and the contours of their yards
had collapsed in the shadows
cast by the streetlights, which
come on by themselves. Who knows
what they've seen in our windows
when they pass, if they are even looking.
They seem intent on walking.
When we see each other, we wave.

There they rest as if they were
the season's meager fruit. Once you begin
to notice them, they turn up everywhere
you go, the boulevard or backyard,
the dog walk or supermarket parking lot,
and lower than you might expect—barely
out of reach—braced in the branches
like frozen balls of knotted twine.

They make you think about yourself,
how your productive work was done
out of sight, camouflaged amid
the foliage of years, protected
and incubated, how it hatched
and, fledged, flew off never to return,
and how mollusks, likewise, live
busy and blind along the ocean's floor
until their tumbling shells wash up
at the braised feet of midwestern visitors,
and then you remember how once those feet were yours.

While she tried
to take her time,
in twenty-five minutes
she devoured
the meal that took
the afternoon to make.
The artichoke with lemon butter,
the chicken in a mushroom sauce,
new potatoes, the crusty bread
to sop up the sauce, a light
dessert of berries and cream,
the wine—gone. All the same,
it took all night to digest.

As if the subject of a portraiture
had come terribly alive
and grabbed hold of the frame
to climb into our world,

so it was the flame
reached out to escape
the confines of an attic window
and gulp the winter night air

before beaten back
by the streams of water
from the hoses on the trucks
whose sirens woke up the neighborhood

to the clawing smoke that by morning
had stained the comfort
of dishes left in the sink a while
and Sunday funnies on the floor.

For Bill Rawlins and Chris Pyle

Liverpool, 1960

I would not have overheard the deal they struck,
the smart one and the cute, freezing out
the quiet one, keeping the songs to themselves.
I'd have been grooming my legs to get to the bits
of decaying biomass lodged on those sticky hairs.

∽

Washington, DC, 1972

The tapping of phones done under crossed cones
of flashlights and the attendant rifling
of files would again have all been lost on me.
The flexing of wings in preparation—one,
now the other—always takes precedence.

∽

Boston, 2001

And so the flash of conspiring glances, connecting
as the flight attendant examined the boarding passes,
would hold not a trace of interest, obviously.
But at the slapping of the tiled wall below me
by the hand of the child impatient to take off,
viewed through the fixed kaleidoscope
of my oblivious eyes—I'm ready to flee.

White grass in the shadows:
you can hear the old men snore
as the geese reclaim the golf course
and the killdeer take the shore.

Unseen by me
are the hidden fishy lives.
The osprey, on the other hand,
looks down, stalls midflight, then dives.

The horses moving through the trees
were like a man determined to endure
the season. Except for the periphery
of leaves, there were no blinders essential
to the withdrawal of the world.

Atop the quivering flesh, the riders appeared
more nearly at home than if on their own two feet.

It didn't matter that I was confused.
That some things are of us but so removed
that they are as foreign as a hand outstretched
in hunger, didn't matter.

Even the forgeries have been authenticated.

The hooves of horses muffled on the path
bore the weight of their riders.
Black hats, black boots slid behind a rock outcropping.
They turned a corner on the trail
and once again came into view.

I want to say I wrote this when
I was young and poor, and that, since then,
I have been out riding.

Yesterday morning, clouds hung low with rain
across our valley, calling to mind the bellies
of slow waves lurching above
the lost ocean floor of deciduous trees.

Later, along the river
I saw a man on the opposite bank
throw a stick into the current, his dog bounding in
to fetch it before it floated downstream.
I was stopped by the pain and panic
as she swam toward the disappearing stick,
fighting her desire to return to her human,
to touch her paws to the silt,
somewhere registering
that the course she was on could bring disaster.

It's been nearly a year since you,
my friend, went under the ocean's immensity,
pulled by your heart
below the glittering quartz face
thundering overhead until the surf
dragged you onto the Hatteras beach.
I have no questions, only a wish,
like one you might have written
on a postcard of a sunny seaside day,
one you didn't send, which is:
"Wish you were here," as trite and true as that.

The little plane is droning overhead.
It circles like someone left alone
on the playground after school
who's found a cinder

near the coal chute
and kicks it to pass the time,
waiting for whomever to remember
to come and take him home. It's practicing.

It crawls from pane to pane, from where I sit,
then heads toward the sun, then turns
in the sky, circles and whines.
Down below—

a quicksilver flash—
a pond edged with cattails
too small for the plane to make them out,
and where the water enters, a stone bridge.

What else is beyond its scope? That there were once
students, canvases, and paints,
considering the bridge
and its reflection.

Real and reflected,
the arches locked like hands,
a half century before the plane
looked down, suspended from a bedroom light.

Tonight, to cover the stench
of my own urine and relieve

the chafe of the catheter bag
tied around my thigh,

I liberally applied
a coat of baby powder

up and down my leg,
casting myself back,

out of the blue, to when
I rubbed the talc on you,

caressing your flesh, turning it
even paler than it was,

the scent rising in a sugary mist,
while you were dying.

Some madeleine, I know.
But still, I hadn't glimpsed

any of that moment since
then, decades now ago,

the soft chalk dusting
the crepe of your skin

doing little of anything
to lessen the terror, nothing

at all to alter fate.
No madeleine, really,

I think now, unsure
as I am, Mother or Father,

which parent you were
I faltered so to nurse.

The hunting château of the king of France:
I picture it then, in 1975—
the walls alive,
sprouting enormous racks,
like dozens of arms, hands,
reaching out to me from the stone blocks,
frozen, locked in place,
cut from the stags cut down in the chase.
There they were after centuries, denied
decomposition that the loam would provide
in due course the undetected living.
They're there today.
Shouldn't they be? Who's to say
all these years, these kings later,
that it should matter
they were preserved in death by sport?
Think of all the wonder they've given
to the countless coming and going since
then like me, a boy wavering like the glass in Chambord,
the hunting château of the king of France.

An invisible cage allows the flock of homing pigeons
to sweep the valley from one side to the other,
the sun trapped on the wings like white sails on a lake.
I've shown you before their billowing flight.

But today I watched them from my window alone,
drawn again, as I am each time they appear,
to their rigorous release, and the way they, unlike you,
wrap themselves in their magnetic return.

I danced on the floating dock
and shook the water hard,
and for a minute each slender reed
of fallen light became a shard.

Two

ELECTION-DAY RACCOON

> To know and not to act is not to
> know at all.
>
> —Japanese proverb

Someone else would have stopped
on the dark November road,
found a weighted limb and clubbed the creature
till it quit its senseless flinching,
trying to right itself
fresh from the rear wheel
of the car in front of me,
trying to get back on its feet,
which clawed the light of my high beams
that caught its blazing eyes.
I chose to leave it to its nature
in its nature, to let it feel itself drain
into the nocturnal loneness that was its life.
I chose for me and my stubborn sentimentality,
more culpable than the unheeding car.
That is who I am. That is what it was.
Campaign signs sprung out of the darkness
along the sides of the road leading back to town,
chanting in their temporary mischief: "Vote Yes," "Vote No."

Now the created soul of man hath also two eyes. The one is the power of seeing into eternity, the other of seeing into time and the creatures, of perceiving how they differ from each other as aforesaid, of giving life and needful things to the body, and ordering and governing it for the best. But these two eyes of the soul of man cannot both perform their work at once; but if the soul shall see with the right eye into eternity, then the left eye must close itself and refrain from working, and be as though it were dead. For if the left eye be fulfilling its office toward outward things, that is, holding converse with time and the creatures, then must the right eye be hindered in its working, that is, in its contemplation. Therefore, whosoever will have the one must let the other go: for "no man can serve two masters."

—*Theologia Germanica*,
trans. S. Winkworth

You say that we are friends
but I've noticed when
you bring your children to my house
they like to play
finders keepers, and you
let them, scolding me
for scolding them to put things
back where they belong.
"You know they'll give them back,"
you tell me. I'm not convinced.
I've watched, reflected in a storefront window,
as your adorable brood
marches out of the shoe store at the mall,
shuffling along in adult high heels

as if the world were their dress-up room.
I've been with you in a Walmart
while you've tried on sunglasses,
cocking them back like a visor
on a knight's helmet
to hold back your hair,
then touring the store as if
they were already yours,
in fact, as if the store were yours,
replacing them not a moment prematurely
before you exited.
I've witnessed in the supermarket
when you've picked up something
you definitely won't use—
chocolate-covered doughnuts or condoms,
for example—and glaring left
and right like a guilty dog, dropped it
in someone else's cart,
then bent down to tie your shoe and walked away.
Where will this lead, I wonder.
Your proprietary nature is riveting.
You've told me how you take a new car for a spin
and drive up to a drive-up window
and place an order to simulate reality—
stimulate reality is more like it.

But I'm the one you make fun of,
availing myself of samples in the farmers' market:
bread, salami, tomatoes, pickled beets,
cheese and fudge, a satisfying breakfast.

Discarded library books, umbrellas
easily inverted to work as intended,
a chair with a missing rung and a sign
saying FREE outside a neighbor's garage,
all find their way to me. Just last week,
a baseball cap liberated by the wind
from the window of a passing pickup
was found skulking in the weeds.
I dusted it off and stuck it in my back pocket.
Who would fare worse in an apocalypse,
when all that is left are our own devices?
After all, the worst that could happen
already would have happened.
I imagine the end of the world
allows for both scavenger and thief:
pickpockets of the dead,
pilferers of the needful things,
the furtive and the self-assured.
Sure, friends it is, then.

Too little oil and
too much soy and heat,
causing the salmon to stick
as I flipped it on its pink side,
the skin ripping from the skillet
and crinkling like foil,
blackened by the cast iron.
But the fish was moist
and buttery and the cat
ate the few fallen splinters
she was offered, dill and all,
and the skin sizzled
and crunched in my mouth
like parchment on which
a message had been written
that I was sworn to protect.

Because he met you at the door,
you offered him the flowers
you'd brought to give the hostess.
Grabbing the stems,
he caught a thorn,
and up popped a bubble of blood
like a ladybug fastened to his fingertip.
Before the two of you knew it
you'd taken his hand
and rushed to stanch the blood
by sucking it between your lips.
That's what you would have done
had it happened to you instead.
He frowned and pulled away
and disappeared to get a bandage,
leaving you alone to hold
the flowers, the roses with which,
an hour before, you'd paced the road
out in the December cold,
waiting for the party to get started.

Ask them anything. They have made
mistakes and have lived in silence
with regrets, although they've kept them
by necessity submerged like swim bladders.

Thirty, forty, fifty years is not too far away
to feel the welts still rising from the lessons
they learned back then. Go ahead—ask them
for advice. They know it's not about them,
despite the fact their answers are. They've known
the gnaw. They're not in need
of anyone's approval or forgiveness
but their own. Their world's reduced
to absence and subsistence.

What urges do they harbor? None
of lasting consequence. A spot of sun,
a breeze, unhurried motion, a bird at the feeder,
a rain gauge, the commentary on the game
from the television in another room,
a cool drink, a light meal when they're feeling peckish.
It seems a degradation of the body and the spirit,
but it's not. It is, in fact, the higher goal, higher
than ambition or some distant calling. Observe
the tugs of guilt and yearning give way to nap.

Isn't this the answer to the sadness
of the waste of lives, the massacres, the wars,
the accidents, the violent endings?
What else is there to want than this
daily excursion, the western window
with its flaming orange and burnt-in blue,
and later on the flickering of the TV screen,
later yet the ankle-high glow of the bathroom nightlight,
and later still the eastern window with its pinkening?

Ask them. They will tell you, if they feel like talking.

Coming home from work, I see
my neighbor on his porch.
His cancer treatment is killing him,
and he's losing his hearing.
Vanity keeps him from shaving off
his silver head of hair.
I join him where he sits
to discuss his day and his discomfort.
Instead, he talks about the time
he fished a lake in Florida
and caught a turtle, hooked her
by the foot, and that old cooter
took that line under the boat
and wrapped it around the anchor rope,
which meant they had to haul
the anchor up and there she was,
as big as a washtub,
hanging by her hind foot,
forcing him to take his knife
and slice the hook from between her toes,
releasing her into the water.
I watch him concentrate
on the cars as they approach
then pass us by, their headlights
nearly useless in the early dusk.
He lets out a fart

and doesn't think I hear.
The air becomes a mist of him,
the chemicals at work, his last meal,
the anti-nausea medication,
a stink of a man, floating away
into the evening air along with
our slender conversation.

The plastic earpiece snapped off your reading glasses.
The strap of your satchel broke at the airport after thirty-six years.
The battery in the kitchen clock ran down. The electricity
in the house flickered off, then back on, resetting the digital time.
The computer acted up, forcing you to reboot repeatedly.
The car began rattling like a can, sidling over the streets of the town.
Moisture came up through the cement garage floor after the rains.
None of this is your fault. The world eventually fails
according to our standards. But what you perceive as failure
is migration, a moving from one state to another. You notice
only the big events, but the change is happening all the time.
The fact these things converge as if in orchestration
on a particularly fraught weekend is the whimsy of physics
that in different circumstances would be considered miraculous.

The hornet's nest at the peak of the tree
is empty of its community. What peers
out like an eye in its ripped mask
is the sky in the shifting west. It cradles
the air that has stung the flaky flask.
Its citizens whose task it was to paste the pulp
into the suspended pavilion now litter the ground
surrounding the tree, buried among the leaves.
Theirs is a quick season.

Which brings me to you, and how this old love,
this new love in age, is like a love in war
and contains war's urgencies, the risks
that won't allow for rational acts,
but is alive by being rash, that will not
wait its due for fear of being done too soon.

I went to get a haircut and my barber shared
the sadness of a tragedy of a well-known client,
a pianist, who after the night's performance
crossed his road to retrieve his mail
and was struck dead by a car, and how the barber
had a few final minutes alone with him to trim
his hair one last time for the viewing. Every time
is the last time. That's what the world keeps teaching.

Let's say the young man stabs the palm
of his own right hand and the blood
floods the intersecting lines
of his "fortune" like a map
and the red hub of all those busy roads
attracts a hummingbird,
which hovers so close
in the leather cage
of his slowly closing hand
he can take its pulse
above the thrum of wings,
and his fingers tighten
till stillness takes the place
of blur and the paradiddle races.
What will it ever think
if he were to let it go?
Will it put the past behind it
and begin its nervous chittering
as it buzzes and swings
in its pendulum dance?
Will it flit to a twig of a high branch
and wait frozen for the air to clear
of terror electrifying the world?
Is this stab and capture worse than walking out
at night and dislodging a brick from an alleyway
and taking it home as ornament
for his own garden wall? Of course it is,
which is why he took the brick.

We heard, I thought, the swelling din
ricochet around the swamp
of waterbirds taking flight,

but nothing in the sky was shaken.
Were they flocks of wild ground fowl,
mutant among the fallen timbers,

convening near the vernal pools
whose jade veneer might mirror for them
unreachable clouds, their wattles and snoods?

Unlikely on all counts, but what
a racket. The squawk and cackle un-
mistakable—except, when we looked, no birds.

We hiked out here when we heard
the diagnosis, but had we heard *that* wrong?
No matter now, or what it was—

we'd suffer through it, even though
suffering was not the most of it.
My only thought was for this diversion

tugging at our sleeves, and how
the underside of camouflage
and mimicry is often thrall.

In truth, the closer to the sound
we crept, the more it died away, like
some roiling unwatched pot removed

from fire cooling to a stop.
As quiet as I thought we'd been,
we'd scared whatever it had been

into hiding and this silence. The bog
and its transparent citizens were still.
The impulse was all or nothing at all.

Soon our focus reverted to
other concerns, and we turned back.
Passing the pools again, we heard a plop.

You listened for a minute to see . . .
but it must have been still too early.
I waited while you caught up with me.

What do you want me to do with the news
now that you've given it to me?
Can we please, for example,
dispense with the talk
of fascists and communists
and who was one or the other,
for a while at least on Sunday afternoon?
Listen. There are birds singing,
and lawn mowers, radios,
and kids on the next block
screaming and laughing.
Maybe they are magnifying the rays
of the sun on the bodies of ants,
but what do you want from me?
Scale back your events,
current, recent, and otherwise,
and reattach the flap of flesh
you've pulled from the face of history.
Stitch it up. Let it heal. The days
are short enough as they are.
We learn, if we're lucky, to be creatures
of the seasons we're meant to be
while it still means something.
As it is, I'm reading the papers
for May 8th and it's June 15th. Please
let me worry instead about the conspiracy

of weeds choking my garden.
The world is turning roughly
a thousand miles an hour.
It's all I can do to stand in place.
Thank you, really, for giving me
the news. Now, please, take it back.

All the kitchen drawers all over the world, with their rubber bands and thumbtacks, postage stamps and twist ties and clipped cartoons, business cards and plumbing receipts, with their seed packets and dried roses, their color swatches and chewing gum, their artist palettes and their unopened letters, calculators and calipers, animal hides and lace trim, false teeth and baby shoes, their foreign coins and their blue jay screeches, buttons and takeout menus, broken marriages and calorie counters, guitar picks and calendars, modeling clay and coat hangers, their exhaust pipes and alarm clocks, early deaths and their paperweights, perfumes and dog collars, step stools and vacuum attachments, their recipes and cut-flower food, their flashlights and souvenirs, and their magnifying glasses and their passwords, their seashells and naps, their frames and blueprints, their shopping lists on the back of envelopes and their restless nights, all, all, all will be emptied one day.

How I loved you because I misremembered you.
Now, you see, I can never go back.
To find what you were is not within
the circus of choice, innuendos
softened once, long since recongealed.
Who but me has torn out
the pages to mark my place?
No one. I rewrite them from memory,
a faulty, selective, mythic thing, a lie,
like saying, "The stars turn into dominos . . ."
as if the sheer sheets of humidity
obscured for my benefit alone
the evening atmosphere smeared across
childhood hilltops the color of melons.

A tree goes down in a summer storm,
half a tree, to be precise, weakened
by heart rot. The lesser side of a sycamore
split and fell from one yard to the next
with a house in its way. No one heard it.
All through this driving rain, this raging
storm, the utility crew feeds the chipper,
sawing off the foliage and limbs,
trying as fast as they can to get it off
the neighbor's house. While we are left
inside without our cable or our internet—
trees will be trees—our only attachment
to the world is the lashing rain, the saws,
the chipper, the generator, all very loud and local.

Except, except, the tree didn't cause the outage,
as it turns out, and the crew are private
contractors hired by the homeowners.
It's only now, after the steam
begins to rise from pockets across the valley
like signal fires, that we venture out
and see that it *was* a sycamore
that exposed the inside of the house,
covered with a blue tarp like the flap
of a robe that almost allows us an eyeful,
or that there *was* any damage at all.

The local is susceptible, it seems,
to the assumptions of the moment.
In retrospect, it's odd that no one heard it.

Picture the woman flat on her back,
dead in the barnyard, laureled with downy feathers,
having tried to dislodge the rock
blocking her from getting her truck
a little closer to the gas tank.
This is the gist of the legacy she's left
to her boys: the one who gets
his riding mower stuck on a root
balanced on a hill. At eighty-four
he falls and breaks a leg—an expensive root—
while trying to pry the tractor loose.
And his brother, hard-headed too,
pruning the churchyard bushes
alone, talking while he works
to his mother, taking advantage
of the morning coolness before he tires.
Think of the hapless chickens.

I cannot conjure a scent the way I can
the sound of squealing tires and thunder,
or the sight of heat lightning and a peeling billboard.
I know the odor of cut grass
and gasoline, of unlit Gauloises,
and wood smoke in the rain.
But I cannot bring them into being.
Standing here in the middle of July,
windows open, with the whir of traffic
like an exhaust fan and evening birds
in electric conversation, I can only sense
what is very close, olfactorily speaking:
the dry dirt from the garden
under my nails, a whiff of sweat,
dead skin, and salt on my hand,
which I bring up to my face, eyes shut, as if
shielding myself from foreign elements
and not as incidental witness to my own life.

Who sits outside my window,
resting on the dead branch
macraméd with vines
(your serious silly head red and rubbery
like alien genitalia),
don't wait for me.
I'm not going anywhere soon.
Dry your wings if you want,
like some farcical symbol
of mock authority, but don't think
hanging around will win you first dibs on me.
I'm not sick or lazy. I'm reading,
which I know sometimes
looks like sleep,
which in turn resembles death.
I understand your confusion.
And seeing you does make me
check my pulse, but it's a nice day,
cool, breezy, few clouds,
and the sky is yours to hang in,
yours for the taking. God, if I could I would.
But since I can't, I'm not ready yet to leave.
See? I'm waving my arms. Your turn.

There are years of mine
for which no record remains,

but one holds out a souvenir
offered from a distant season: horses

huddled in a hillside pasture
amid patches of old snow

behind acres of white fences.
How long we must have stood there

muffled in the crystalline fog,
considering each other from afar.

Yet at some point, long ago,
spurred by the snow starting again

or the growing dark and chill,
I decided I'd had enough

and headed toward the family car,
its heater and headlights and radio,

its promise of escape from escape,
parked on the side of the road.

Some of them began to nuzzle the ground.
A few wandered back to their trough.

REASONS NOT TO LEAVE

> What becomes of the heart of a hollow tree?
>
> —George Stimpson,
> *A Book about a Thousand Things*

He thought of returning to a home he knew was gone.
His object: to find the tree on which he'd carved
his initials with those of his love inside a heart.
But in the midst of plotting the trip, he was stopped
by the fear of forgetting where the tree had stood,
and if he remembered, would it still be there,
and if it were there, would the bark have blistered
and scarred over the heart, obscuring the letters,
and if the letters were legible, would he
know what they stood for, would he recall
her name after such a long time? Instead of leaving,
he's drawn to an elm visible from his front stoop,
and follows the map of the rough trunk with his hands,
inventing the wrinkles, the shape of an aged face
in the tree's dark ligatures, saving himself going
two hundred miles to the north—to where?—
and two hundred miles back, chiseling the bark.

Word arrives from acquaintances
bewildered that you have turned away
from our youthful ideologies,
and they wonder what there is of you to salvage.
What is different since last we talked?

The jets have disappeared from the sky
and the clouds moved in, scraping
the tops of cell towers as if
in search of their mooring lines.
But we are the ones unmoored.

Long ago I wrote to you in another poem,
feeling the sting of the miles between us.
Once, you braided your words
like tendrils around your melodies
and our small world was in your pocket.
Abracadabra. Legerdemain.

The friends who left us in passing years
without pretense or fanfare stay
silent and unsurprised.
                              I imagine
it wouldn't have mattered, but I should
have sent that poem off to you
before the distances had dulled
and nothing offered felt forbidden.

How can I enter, having been here
the entire time? If others see me,
like the cloud-spun moon that catches
their sleepless eyes, it's all their doing.
At the end, to them I seemed, at best,
a litany of silence on silence,
a series of recedings, a diet
of small erasures. I'm fine with that.
Relinquishing the narrow streets
to the colonizers of the present
was small potatoes, as they say,
against the bleaching of my deeds,
which happens faster than they know,
a whole other freedom there—a release
one learns to savor in the fullness of time.
This gradual vanishing quiets the spirit;
it turns us feral, embracing the wild
as the new dispensation, the sleeping alone
out of doors—because why not?—
tasting the voided world unbridled
without interaction, a constant sidestepping.
Take, for example, in the grocery store:
a former colleague will reach past
your shoulder to grab a can of beans,
wrinkling his quizzical nose as the scent
of inevitable contagion wafts by.

It's almost funny, so you almost laugh.
Granted, there are times walking the trails
I catch sight of a stranger on a parallel path
who stops and stares in my direction,
forcing me to find the underbrush
like a coywolf, shaking off
whatever it was that gave me away.
In all likelihood, it was that he
was ripening for removal and, unbeknownst
to himself, was starting to recede—
joining us wayposts of the forgettable.
As for this entering—I've no control
over it. It's all on them, the others.
That said, better you not think of me
as just there—beyond your field of vision.
For all it matters, I am not there,
or here, past their dumbshow grasp
until they truly grasp. Remember this:
there's levity in almost every loss.
And remember me. [*Exit* GHOST.]

You wake up because
you think there are squirrels
in the walls. You can hear their feet.

It's not squirrels. It's sleet.

You wake again as the frequency increases.
The skillet in the kitchen is sizzling
on the stove. You listen.

You live alone. Still sleet.

Finally you rise and see the world is
insulated with a sheet
of ice. Glistening paralysis.

Now you can breathe unafraid.
It's a better world than the ones you made.